W9-AAT-430

Jane Goodall
and the
Chimpanzees

By LARA AVERY

Illustrated by MARCIN PIWOWARSKI

CANTATA
LEARNING
MANKATO, MINNESOTA

CANTATA LEARNING

MANKATO, MINNESOTA

Published by Cantata Learning
1710 Roe Crest Drive
North Mankato, MN 56003
www.cantatalearning.com

Library of Congress Control Number: 2014938336
ISBN: 978-1-63290-082-1

Jane Goodall and the Chimpanzees by Lara Avery
Illustrated by Marcin Piwowarski

Book design by Tim Palin Creative
Music produced by Wes Schuck
Audio recorded, mixed, and mastered at Two Fish Studios, Mankato, MN

Printed in the United States of America.

♪ VISIT ♫

WWW.CANTATALEARNING.COM/ACCESS-OUR-MUSIC

4

Jane Goodall
(Born 1934)

Jane Goodall is a special kind of scientist called a "primatologist." This means that she is an expert on the **behavior**, diet, and **habitat** of **primates**. Primates are a large group of **mammals** that include monkeys, apes, baboons, gorillas, orangutans, and Jane's favorite, **chimpanzees**. Jane moved from England to Africa to study the behavior of chimpanzees.

We have always loved
animals. Yes, it's true.

But we never thought
they loved like I love you.

We trained them, worked
them, put them in a zoo,

and never saw them in
the light that I see you.

Doctor Jane, far from home, in a **Tanzanian** tree.

No one saw what she saw in a chimpanzee.

She didn't poke, pull, prod, or cage them.
She knew that they were clever too.

She saw them in the light that I see you.

Everybody's in the light that I see you,
with smiles and tears and jobs to do.

Mammals walk and talk in different ways,

but they love each other just the same.

Some chimpanzees want a treat.

We never thought that they'd eat meat.

But Jane watched the chimps at feeding time.

They ate juicy bugs full of slime.

They have homes and neighborhoods in the trees.

They fight and forgive like family.

Jane gave them names like Mike, Fifi,

David, Graybeard, Flint, and Humphrey.

They saw her in the light that you see me.

Everybody's in the light that I see you,
with smiles and tears and jobs to do.
Mammals walk and talk in different ways,
but they love each other just the same.

When Jane came back, the world had changed.

Everybody's trying to **advocate**

for the rights of chimps to be safe and to be treated

like the friends they are, and you could lead it.

Everybody's in the light that I see you,
with smiles and tears and jobs to do.
Mammals walk and talk in different ways,
but they love each other just the same.

21

GLOSSARY

advocate—a person who supports an idea or plan

behavior—the way a person or animal acts

chimpanzee—a large primate without a tail

habitat—the natural place and conditions in which a plant or animal lives

mammal—a warm–blooded animal that breathes air

primate—any member of the group of intelligent animals that includes humans, apes, and monkeys

Tanzania—a country in the southern part of Africa

Jane Goodall and the Chimpanzees

Lara Avery

Indie Rock

ACTIVITY QUESTIONS

1. What's your favorite animal?

2. What does it eat?

3. Draw a picture of the animal.

TO LEARN MORE

Edison, Erin. *Jane Goodall*. Mankato, MN: Capstone Press, 2013.

McDonnell, Patrick. *Me… Jane*. New York: Little, Brown, 2011.

Winter, Jeanette. *The Watcher: Jane Goodall's Life with the Chimps*. New York: Random House, 2011.

Zobel, Derek. *Chimpanzees*. Minneapolis, MN: Bellwether Media, 2012.

DISCOVERING SCIENCE

ELECTRICITY AND MAGNETISM

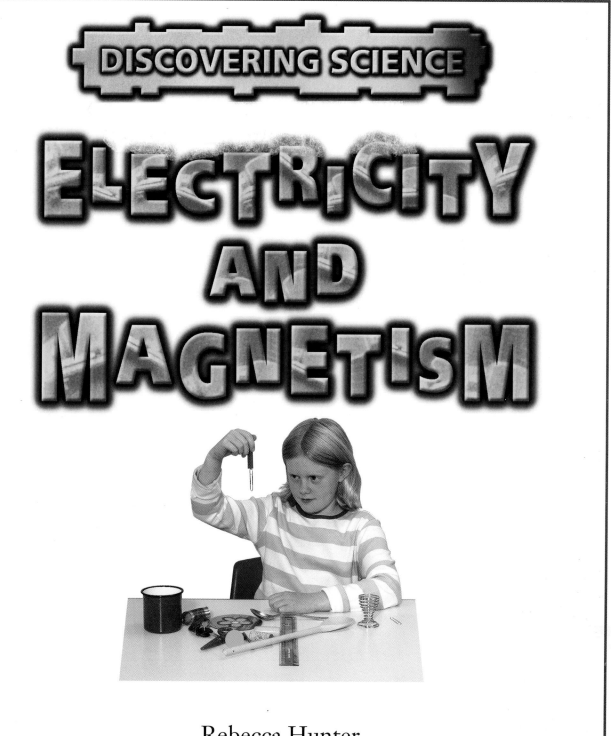

Rebecca Hunter

www.raintreepublishers.co.uk
Visit our website to find out more information about **Raintree** books.

To order:
☎ Phone 44 (0) 1865 888112
🖹 Send a fax to 44 (0) 1865 314091
💻 Visit the Raintree Bookshop at www.raintreepublishers.co.uk to browse our catalogue and order online.

First published in Great Britain by Raintree,
Halley Court, Jordan Hill, Oxford
OX2 8EJ, part of Harcourt Education.

Raintree is a registered trademark of Harcourt
Education Ltd.

Produced for Raintree by Discovery Books Ltd
Design: Ian Winton
Editorial: Rebecca Hunter
Consultant: Jeremy Bloomfield
Commissioned photography: Chris Fairclough
Illustrations: Keith Williams, Joanna Williams and Stefan
Chabluk
Production: Jonathan Smith

Originated by Dot Gradations Ltd
Printed and bound in China by South China
  Printing Company

ISBN 1 844 21566 0 (hardback)
07 06 05 04 03
10 9 8 7 6 5 4 3 2 1

ISBN 1 844 21573 3 (paperback)
08 07 06 05 04
10 9 8 7 6 5 4 3 2 1

British Library Cataloguing in Publication Data
Hunter, Rebecca
Electricity and Magnetism. – (Discovering Science)
537

A full catalogue record for this book is available from the
British Library.

Acknowledgements
The publishers would like to thank the following for
permission to reproduce photographs:
Beamish Museum: page **4**; Chris Fairclough: page **7, 13**;
Discovery Picture Library: page **9** top, **20, 25, 27**; Edison
Mission Energy: page **17, 18**; Science Photo Library:
page **15** (Kent Wood), **19** (Russel D Curtis), **29** (Alex
Bartcl); gcttyonc Stonc: pagc **5** top (Cosmo Condina),
bottom (David Young Wolff), **9** bottom (Doug Armand),
11 (Paul Dance), **16** (Ken Biggs).

Cover photograph of electricity pylon reproduced with
permission of Science Photo Library.

The publishers would like to thank the following schools
for their help in providing equipment, models and
locations for photography sessions: Bedstone College,
Bucknell, Moor Park, Ludlow and Packwood Haugh,
Shrewsbury.

Every effort has been made to contact copyright holders
of any material reproduced in this book.
Any omissions will be rectified in subsequent printings if
notice is given to the publishers.

Any words appearing in the text in bold, **like
this**, are explained in the Glossary.